WITH THE
TURKS
IN PALESTINE

ALEXANDER AARONSOHN

1st WORLD
LIBRARY
Literary Society

With The Turks in Palestine

Alexander Aaronsohn

© 1st World Library – Literary Society, 2004
PO Box 2211
Fairfield, IA 52556
www.1stworldlibrary.org
First Edition

LCCN: 2004195190

Softcover ISBN: 1-4218-0100-0
Hardcover ISBN: 1-4218-0000-4
eBook ISBN: 1-4218-0200-7

Purchase *"With The Turks in Palestine"*
as a traditional bound book at:
www.1stWorldLibrary.org/purchase.asp?ISBN=1-4218-0100-0

1st World Library Literary Society is a nonprofit organization dedicated to promoting literacy by:

- Creating a free internet library accessible from any computer worldwide.
- Hosting writing competitions and offering book publishing scholarships.

Readers interested in supporting literacy through sponsorship, donations or membership please contact:
literacy@1stworldlibrary.org
Check us out at: www.1stworldlibrary.ORG
and start downloading free ebooks today.

With The Turks in Palestine
contributed by Tim, Ed & Rodney
in support of
1st World Library Literary Society

TO MY MOTHER

WHO LIVED AND FOUGHT AND DIED
FOR A REGENERATED PALESTINE

What have I done, or tried, or said
In thanks to that dear woman dead?

MASEFIELD

ACKNOWLEDGMENT

To the editors of the *Atlantic Monthly*, to the publishers, and to the many friends who have encouraged me, I am and shall ever remain grateful

CONTENTS

INTRODUCTION

While Belgium is bleeding and hoping, while Poland suffers and dreams of liberation, while Serbia is waiting for redemption, there is a little country the soul of which is torn to pieces - a little country that is so remote, so remote that her ardent sighs cannot be heard.

It is the country of perpetual sacrifice, the country that saw Abraham build the altar upon which he was ready to immolate his only son, the country that Moses saw from a distance, stretching in beauty and loveliness, - a land of promise never to be attained, - the country that gave the world its symbols of soul and spirit. Palestine!

No war correspondents, no Red Cross or relief committees have gone to Palestine, because no actual fighting has taken place there, and yet hundreds of thousands are suffering there that worst of agonies, the agony of the spirit.

Those who have devoted their lives to show the world that Palestine can be made again a country flowing with milk and honey, those who have dreamed of reviving the spirit of the prophets and the great teachers, are hanged and persecuted and exiled, their dreams shattered, their holy places profaned, their work ruined. Cut off from the world, with no bread to sustain the starving body, the heavy boot of a barbarian soldiery trampling their very soul, the dreamers of Palestine refuse to surrender, and amidst the clash of guns and swords they are battling for the spirit with the weapons of the spirit.

The time has not yet come to write the record of these battles, nor even to attempt to render justice to the sublime heroes of Palestine. This book is merely the story of some of the personal experiences of one who has done less and suffered less than thousands of his comrades.

ALEXANDER AARONSOHN

CHAPTER I

ZICRON-JACOB

Thirty-five years ago, the impulse which has since been organized as the Zionist Movement led my parents to leave their homes in Roumania and emigrate to Palestine, where they joined a number of other Jewish pioneers in founding Zicron-Jacob - a little village lying just south of Mount Carmel, in that fertile coastal region close to the ancient Plains of Armageddon.

Here I was born; my childhood was passed here in the peace and harmony of this little agricultural community, with its whitewashed stone houses huddled close together for protection against the native Arabs who, at first, menaced the life of the new colony. The village was far more suggestive of Switzerland than of the conventional slovenly villages of the East, mud-built and filthy; for while it was the purpose of our people, in returning to the Holy Land, to foster the Jewish language and the social conditions of the Old Testament as far as possible, there was nothing retrograde in this movement. No time was lost in introducing progressive methods of agriculture, and the climatological experiments of other countries were observed and made use of in developing the ample natural resources of the land.

Eucalyptus, imported from Australia, soon gave the shade of its cool, healthful foliage where previously no trees had grown. In the course of time dry farming (which some people consider a recent discovery, but which in reality is as old as the Old Testament) was introduced and extended with American agricultural implements; blooded cattle were imported, and poultry-raising on a large scale was undertaken with the aid of incubators - to the disgust of the Arabs, who look on such usurpation of the hen's functions as against nature and sinful. Our people replaced the wretched native trails with good roads, bordered by hedges of thorny acacia which, in season, were covered with downy little yellow blossoms that smelled sweeter than honey when the sun was on them.

More important than all these, a communistic village government was established, in which both sexes enjoyed equal rights, including that of suffrage - strange as this may seem to persons who (when they think of the matter at all) form vague conceptions of all the women-folk of Palestine as shut up in harems.

A short experience with Turkish courts and Turkish justice taught our people that they would have to establish a legal system of their own; two collaborating judges were therefore appointed - one to interpret the Mosaic law, another to temper it with modern jurisprudence. All Jewish disputes were settled by this court. Its effectiveness may be judged by the fact that the Arabs, weary of Turkish venality, - as open and shameless as anywhere in the world, - began in increasing numbers to bring their difficulties to our tribunal. Jews are law-abiding people, and life in those Palestine colonies tended to bring out the fraternal qualities of our race; but it is interesting to note that in over thirty years not one Jewish criminal case was reported from forty-five villages.

Zicron-Jacob was a little town of one hundred and thirty "fires" - so we call it - when, in 1910, on the advice of my elder brother, who was head of the Jewish Experiment Station at Athlit, an ancient town of the Crusaders, I left for America to enter the service of the United States in the Department of Agriculture. A few days after reaching this country I took out my first naturalization papers and proceeded to Washington, where I became part of that great government service whose beneficent activity is too little known by Americans. Here I remained until June, 1913, when I returned to Palestine with the object of taking motion-pictures and stereopticon views. These I intended to use in a lecturing tour for spreading the Zionist propaganda in the United States.

During the years of my residence in America, I was able to appreciate and judge in their right value the beauty and inspiration of the life which my people led in the Holy Land. From a distance, too, I saw better the need for organization among our communities, and I determined to build up a fraternal union of the young Jewish men all over the country.

Two months after my return from America, an event occurred which gave impetus to these projects. The physician of our village, an old man who had devoted his entire life to serving and healing the people of Palestine, without distinction of race or religion, was driving home one evening in his carriage from a neighboring settlement. With him was a young girl of sixteen. In a deserted place they were set upon by four armed Arabs, who beat the old man to unconsciousness as he tried, in vain, to defend the girl from the terrible fate which awaited her.

Night came on. Alarmed by the absence of the physician, we young men rode out in search of him. We finally discovered what had happened; and then and there, in the serene moonlight of that Eastern night, with tragedy close at hand, I made my comrades take oath on the honor of their sisters to organize themselves into a strong society for the defense of the life and honor of our villagers and of our people at large.

These details are, perhaps, useful for the better understanding of the disturbances that came thick and fast when in August, 1914, the war-madness broke out among the nations of Europe. The repercussion was at once felt even in our remote corner of the earth. Soon after the German invasion of Belgium the Turkish army was mobilized and all citizens of the Empire between nineteen and forty-five years were called to the colors. As the Young Turk Constitution of 1909 provided that all Christians and Jews were equally liable to military service, our young men knew that they, too, would be called upon to make the common sacrifice. For the most part, they were not unwilling to sustain the Turkish Government. While the Constitution imposed on them the burden of militarism, it had brought with it the compensation of freedom of religion and equal rights; and we could not forget that for six hundred years Turkey has held her gates wide open to the Jews who fled from the Spanish Inquisition and similar ministrations of other civilized countries.

Of course, we never dreamed that Turkey would do anything but remain neutral. If we had had any idea of the turn things were ultimately to take, we should have given a different greeting to the *mouchtar*, or sheriff, who came to our village with the list of mobilizable men to be called on for service. My own position was a curious one. I had every intention of completing the process of becoming an American citizen, which I had begun by taking out "first papers." In the eyes of the law, however, I was still a Turkish subject, with no claim to American protection. This was sneeringly pointed out to me by the American Consul at Haifa, who happens to be a German; so there was no other course but to surrender myself to the Turkish Government.

CHAPTER II

PRESSED INTO THE SERVICE

There was no question as to my eligibility for service. I was young and strong and healthy - and even if I had not been, the physical examination of Turkish recruits is a farce. The enlisting officers have a theory of their own that no man is really unfit for the army - a theory which has been fostered by the ingenious devices of the Arabs to avoid conscription. To these wild people the protracted discipline of military training is simply a purgatory, and for weeks before the recruiting officers are due, they dose themselves with powerful herbs and physics and fast, and nurse sores into being, until they are in a really deplorable condition. Some of them go so far as to cut off a finger or two. The officers, however, have learned to see beyond these little tricks, and few Arabs succeed in wriggling through their drag-net. I have watched dozens of Arabs being brought in to the recruiting office on camels or horses, so weak were they, and welcomed into the service with a severe beating - the sick and the shammers sharing the same fate. Thus it often happens that some of the new recruits die after their first day of garrison life.

Together with twenty of my comrades, I presented myself at the recruiting station at Acco (the St. Jean d'Acre of history). We had been given to understand that, once our names were registered, we should be allowed to return home to provide ourselves with money, suitable clothing, and food, as well as to bid our families good-bye. To our astonishment, however, we were marched off to the Hân, or caravanserai, and locked into the great courtyard with hundreds of dirty Arabs. Hour after hour passed; darkness came, and finally we had to stretch ourselves on the ground and make the best of a bad situation. It was a night of horrors. Few of us had closed an eye when, at dawn, an officer appeared and ordered us out of the Hân. From our total number about three hundred (including four young men from our village and myself) were picked out and told to make ready to start at once for Saffêd, a town in the hills of northern Galilee near the Sea of Tiberias, where our garrison was to be located. No attention was paid to our requests that we be allowed to return to our homes for a final visit. That same morning we were on our way to Saffêd - a motley, disgruntled crew.

It was a four days' march - four days of heat and dust and physical suffering. The September sun smote us mercilessly as we straggled along the miserable native trail, full of gullies and loose stones. It would not have been so bad if we had been adequately shod or clothed; but soon we found ourselves envying the ragged Arabs as they trudged along barefoot, paying no heed to the jagged flints. (Shoes, to the Arab, are articles for ceremonious indoor use; when any serious walking is to be done, he takes them off, slings them over his shoulder, and trusts to the horny soles of his feet.)

To add to our troubles, the Turkish officers, with characteristic fatalism, had made no commissary provision for us whatever. Any food we ate had to be purchased by the roadside from our own funds, which were scant enough to start with. The Arabs were in a terrible plight. Most of them were penniless, and, as the pangs of hunger set in, they began pillaging right and left from the little farms by the wayside. From modest beginnings - poultry and vegetables - they progressed to larger game, unhindered by the officers. Houses were entered, women insulted; time and again I saw a stray horse, grazing by the roadside, seized by a crowd of grinning Arabs, who piled on the poor beast's back until he was almost crushed to earth, and rode off triumphantly, while their comrades held back the weeping owner. The result of this sort of "requisitioning," was that our band of recruits was followed by an increasing throng of farmers - imploring, threatening, trying by hook or by crook to win back the stolen goods. Little satisfaction did they get, although some of them went with us as far as Saffêd.

Our garrison town is not an inviting place, nor has it an inviting reputation. Lord Kitchener himself had good reason to remember it. As a young lieutenant of twenty-three, in the Royal Engineering Corps, he was nearly killed there by a band of fanatical Arabs while surveying for the Palestine Exploration Fund. Kitchener had a narrow escape of it (one of his fellow officers was shot dead close by him), but he went calmly ahead and completed his maps, splendid large-scale affairs which have never since been equaled - and which are now in use by the Turkish and German armies! However, though Saffêd combines most of the unpleasant characteristics of Palestine native towns, we welcomed the sight of it, for we were used up by the march. An old deserted mosque was given us for barracks; there, on the bare stone floor, in close-packed promiscuity, too tired to react to filth and vermin, we spent our first night as soldiers of the Sultan, while the milky moonlight streamed in through every chink and aperture, and bats flitted round the vaulting above the snoring carcasses of the recruits.

Next morning we were routed out at five. The black depths of the well in the center of the mosque courtyard provided doubtful water for washing, bathing, and drinking; then came breakfast, - our first government meal, - consisting, simply enough, of boiled rice, which was ladled out into tin wash-basins holding rations for ten men. In true Eastern fashion we squatted down round the basin and dug into the rice with our fingers. At first I was rather upset by this sort of table manners, and for some time I ate with my eyes fixed on my own portion, to avoid seeing the Arabs, who fill the palms of their hands with rice, pat it into a ball and cram it into their mouths just so, the bolus making a great lump in their lean throats as it reluctantly descends.

In the course of that same morning we were allotted our uniforms. The Turkish uniform, under indirect German influence, has been greatly modified during the past five years. It is of khaki - a greener khaki than that of the British army, and of conventional European cut. Spiral puttees and good boots are provided; the only peculiar feature is the headgear - a curious, uncouth-looking combination of the turban and the German helmet, devised by Enver Pasha to combine religion and practicality, and called in his honor *enverieh*. (With commendable thrift, Enver patented his invention, and it is rumored that he has drawn a comfortable fortune from its sale.) An excellent uniform it is, on the whole; but, to our disgust, we found that in the great olive-drab pile to which we were led, there was not a single new one. All were old, discarded, and dirty, and the mere thought of putting on the clothes of some unknown Arab legionary, who, perhaps, had died of cholera at Mecca or Yemen, made me shudder. After some indecision, my friends and I finally went up to one of the officers and offered to *buy* new uniforms with the money we expected daily from our families. The officer, scenting the chance for a little private profit, gave his consent.

The days and weeks following were busy ones. From morning till night, it was drill, drill, and again drill. We were divided into groups of fifty, each of which was put in charge of a young non-commissioned officer from the Military School of Constantinople or Damascus, or of some Arab who had seen several years' service. These instructors had a hard time of it; the German military system, which had only recently been introduced, was too much for them. They kept mixing up the old and the new methods of training, with the result that it was often hopeless to try and make out their orders. Whole weeks were spent in grinding into the Arabs the names of the different parts of the rifle; weeks more went to teaching them to clean it - although it must be said that, once they had mastered these technicalities, they were excellent shots. Their efficiency would have been considerably greater if there had been more target-shooting. From the very first, however, we felt that there was a scarcity of ammunition. This shortage the drill-masters, in a spirit of compensation, attempted to make up by abundant severity. The whip of soft, flexible, stinging leather, which seldom leaves the Turkish officer's hand, was never idle. This was not surprising, for the Arab is a cunning fellow, whose only respect is for brute force. He exercises it himself on every possible victim, and expects the same treatment from his superiors.

So far as my comrades and I were concerned, I must admit that we were generally treated kindly. We knew most of the drill-exercises from the gymnastic training we had practiced since childhood, and the officers realized that we were educated and came from respectable families. The same was also true with regard to the native Christians, most of whom can read and write and are of a better class than the Mohammedans of the country. When Turkey threw in her lot with the Germanic powers, the attitude toward the Jews and Christians changed radically; but of this I shall speak later.

It was a hard life we led while in training at Saffêd; evening would find us dead tired, and little disposed for anything but rest. As the tremendous light-play of the Eastern sunsets faded away, we would gather in little groups in the courtyard of our mosque - its minaret towering black against a turquoise sky - and talk fitfully of the little happenings of the day, while the Arabs murmured gutturally around us. Occasionally, one of them would burst into a quavering, hot-blooded tribal love-song. It happened that I was fairly well known among these natives through my horse Kochba - of pure Maneghi-Sbeli blood - which I had purchased from some Anazzi Bedouins who were encamped not far from Aleppo: a swift and intelligent animal he was, winner of many races, and in a land where a horse is considerably more valuable than a wife, his ownership cast quite a glamour over me.

In the evenings, then, the Arabs would come up to chat. As they speak seldom of their children, of their women-folk never, the conversation was limited to generalities about the crops and the weather, or to the recitation of never-ending tales of Abou-Zeid, the famous hero of the Beni-Hilal, or of Antar the glorious. Politics, of which they have amazing ideas, also came in for discussion. Napoleon Bonaparte and Queen Victoria are still living figures to them; but (significantly enough) they considered the Kaiser king of all the kings of this world, with the exception of the Sultan, whom they admitted to equality.

Seldom did an evening pass without a dance. As darkness fell, the Arabs would gather in a great circle around one of their comrades, who squatted on the ground with a bamboo flute; to a weird minor music they would begin swaying and moving about while some self-chosen poet among them would sing impromptu verses to the flute *obbligato*. As a rule the themes were homely.

"To-morrow we shall eat rice and meat," the singer would wail.

"*Yaha lili-amali*" (my endeavor be granted), came the full-throated response of all the others. The chorus was tremendously effective. Sometimes the singer would indulge in pointed personalities, with answering roars of laughter.

These dances lasted for hours, and as they progressed the men gradually worked themselves up into a frenzy. I never failed to wonder at these people, who, without the aid of alcohol, could reproduce the various stages of intoxication. As I lay by and watched the moon riding serenely above these frantic men and their twisting black shadows, I reflected that they were just in the condition when one word from a holy man would suffice to send them off to wholesale murder and rapine.

It was my good fortune soon to be released from the noise and dirt of the mosque. I had had experience with corruptible Turkish officers; and one day, when barrack conditions became unendurable, I went to the officer commanding our division - an old Arab from Latakieh who had been called from retirement at the time of the mobilization. He lived in a little tent near the mosque, where I found him squatting on the floor, nodding drowsily over his comfortable paunch. As he was an officer of the old régime, I entered boldly, squatted beside him and told him my troubles. The answer came with an enormous shrug of the shoulders.

"You are serving the Sultan. Hardship should be sweet!"

"I should be more fit to serve him if I got more sleep and rest."

He waved a fat hand about the tent.

"Look at me! Here I am, an officer of rank and" - shooting a knowing look at me - "I have not even a nice blanket."

"A crime! A crime!" I interrupted. "To think of it, when I, a humble soldier, have dozens of them at home! I should be honored if you would allow me - " My voice trailed off suggestively.

"How could you get one?" he asked.

"Oh, I have friends here in Saffêd but I *must* be able to sleep in a nice place."

"Of course; certainly. What would you suggest?"

"That hotel kept by the Jewish widow might do," I replied.

More amenities were exchanged, the upshot of which was that my four friends and I were given permission to sleep at the inn - a humble place, but infinitely better than the mosque. It was all perfectly simple.

Alexander Aaronsohn

CHAPTER III

THE GERMAN PROPAGANDA

So passed the days of our training, swiftly, mono-
tonously, until the fateful December morning when the
news came like a thunderbolt that Turkey was about to
join hands with Germany. We had had reports of the
war - of a kind. Copies of telegrams from Constantinople, printed in Arabic, were circulated among us,
giving accounts of endless German victories. These,
however, we had laughed at as fabrications of a
Prussophile press agency, and in our skepticism we
had failed to give the Teutons credit for the successes
they had actually won. To us, born and bred in the East
as we were, the success of German propaganda in the
Turkish Empire could not come as an overwhelming
surprise; but its fullness amazed us.

It may be of timely interest to say a few words here
regarding this propaganda as I have seen it in
Palestine, spreading under strong and efficient
organization for twenty years.

In order to realize her imperialistic dreams, Germany
absolutely needed Palestine. It was the key to the
whole Oriental situation. No mere coincidence brought
the Kaiser to Damascus in November, 1898, - the same
month that Kitchener, in London, was hailed as

Gordon's avenger, - when he uttered his famous phrase at the tomb of Saladin: "Tell the three hundred million Moslems of the world that I am their friend!" We have all seen photographs of the imperial figure, draped in an amazing burnous of his own designing (above which the Prussian *Pickelhaube* rises supreme), as he moved from point to point in this portentous visit: we may also have seen Caran d'Ache's celebrated cartoon (a subject of diplomatic correspondence) representing this same imperial figure, in its Oriental toggery, riding into Jerusalem on an ass.

The nations of Europe laughed at this visit and its transparent purpose, but it was all part of the scheme which won for the Germans the concessions for the Konia-Bagdad Railway, and made them owners of the double valley of the Euphrates and Tigris. Through branch lines projected through the firman, they are practically in control of both the Syrian routes toward the Cypriotic Mediterranean and the Lebanon valleys. They also control the three Armenian routes of Cappadocia, the Black Sea, and the trans-Caucasian branch of Urfa, Marach, and Mardine. (The fall of Erzerum has altered conditions respecting this last.) They dominate the Persian routes toward Tauris and Teheran as well; and last, but not least, the Gulf branch of Zobeir. These railways delivered into German hands the control of Persia, whence the road to India may be made easy: through Syria lies the route to the Suez Canal and Egypt, which was used in February, 1915, and will probably be used again this year.

To make this Oriental dream a reality, the Germans have not relied on their railway concessions alone. Their Government has done everything in its power to encourage German colonization in Palestine. Scattered all over the country are German mills that half of the time have nothing to grind. German hotels have been opened in places seldom frequented by tourists. German engineers appeared in force, surveying, sounding, noting. All these colonists held gatherings in the Arab villages, when the ignorant natives were told of the greatness of Germany, of her good intentions, and of the evil machinations of other powers. What I state here can be corroborated by any one who knows Palestine and has lived in it.

About the time when we first knew that Turkey would join the Germanic powers came the news that the "Capitulations" had been revoked. As is generally known, foreigners formerly enjoyed the protection of their respective consuls. The Turkish Government, under the terms of the so-called Capitulations, or agreements, had no jurisdiction over an American, for instance, or a Frenchman, who could not be arrested without the consent of his consul. In the Ottoman Empire, where law and justice are not at a premium, such protection was a wholesome and necessary policy.

The revoking of the Capitulations was a terrible blow to all the Europeans, meaning, as it did, the practical abolition of all their rights. Upon the Arabs it acted like an intoxicant. Every boot-black or boatman felt that he was the equal of the accursed Frank, who now had no consul to protect him; and abuses began immediately. Moreover, as if by magic, the whole country became Germanized. In all the mosques, Friday prayers were ended with an invocation for the welfare of the Sultan and "Hadji Wilhelm." The significance of this lies in the fact that the title "Hadji" can be properly applied only to a Moslem who has made the pilgrimage to Mecca and kissed the sacred stone of the Kaaba. Instant death is the penalty paid by any Christian who is found within that enclosure: yet Wilhelm II, head of the Lutheran faith, stepped forward as "Hadji Wilhelm." His pictures were sold everywhere; German officers appeared; and it seemed as if a wind of brutal mastery were blowing.

The dominant figure of this movement in Palestine was, without doubt, the German Consul at Haifa, Leutweld von Hardegg. He traveled about the country, making speeches, and distributing pamphlets in Arabic, in which it was elaborately proved that Germans are not Christians, like the French or English, but that they are descendants of the prophet Mohammed. Passages from the Koran were quoted, prophesying the coming of the Kaiser as the Savior of Islam.

CHAPTER IV

ROAD-MAKING AND DISCHARGE

The news of the actual declaration of war by Turkey caused a tremendous stir in our regiment. The prevailing feeling was one of great restlessness and discontent. The Arabs made many bitter remarks against Germany. "Why didn't she help us against the Italians during the war for Tripoli?" they said. "Now that she is in trouble she is drawing us into the fight." Their opinions, however, soon underwent a change. In the first place, they came to realize that Turkey had taken up arms against Russia; and Russia is considered first and foremost the arch-enemy. German reports of German successes also had a powerful effect on them. They began to grow boastful, arrogant; and the sight of the plundering of Europeans, Jews, and Christians convinced them that a very desirable régime was setting in. Saffêd has a large Jewish colony, and it was torment for me to have to witness the outrages that my people suffered in the name of "requisitioning."

The final blow came one morning when all the Jewish and Christian soldiers of our regiment were called out and told that henceforth they were to serve in the *taboor amlieh*, or working corps. The object of this action, plainly enough, was to conciliate and flatter the Mohammedan population, and at the same time to put the Jews and Christians, who for the most part favored the cause of the Allies, in a position where they would be least dangerous. We were disarmed; our uniforms were taken away, and we became hard-driven "gangsters." I shall never forget the humiliation of that day when we, who, after all, were the best-disciplined troops of the lot, were first herded to our work of pushing wheelbarrows and handling spades, by grinning Arabs, rifle on shoulder. We were set to building the road between Saffêd and Tiberias, on the Sea of Galilee - a link in the military highway from Damascus to the coast, which would be used for the movement of troops in case the railroad should be cut off. It had no immediate strategic bearing on the attack against Suez, however.

From six in the morning till seven at night we were hard at it, except for one hour's rest at noon. While we had money, it was possible to get some slight relief by bribing our taskmasters; but this soon came to an end, and we had to endure their brutality as best we could. The wheelbarrows we used were the property of a French company which, before the war, was undertaking a highway to Beirut. No grease was provided for the wheels, so that there was a maddening squeaking and squealing in addition to the difficulty of pushing the barrows. One day I suggested to an inspection officer that if the wheels were not greased the axles would be burned out. He agreed with me and issued an order that the men were to provide their own oil to lubricate the wheels!

I shall not dwell on the physical sufferings we underwent while working on this road, for the reason that the conditions I have described were prevalent over the whole country; and later, when I had the

Alexander Aaronsohn

opportunity to visit some construction camps in Samaria and Judaea found that in comparison our lot had been a happy one. While we were breaking stones and trundling squeaking wheelbarrows, however, the most disquieting rumors began to drift in to us from our home villages. Plundering had been going on in the name of "requisitioning"; the country was full of soldiery whose capacity for mischief-making was well known to us, and it was torture to think of what might be happening in our peaceful homes where so few men had been left for protection. All the barbed-wire fences, we heard, had been torn up and sent north for the construction of barricades. In a wild land like Palestine, where the native has no respect for property, where fields and crops are always at the mercy of marauders, the barbed-wire fence has been a tremendous factor for civilization, and with these gone the Arabs were once more free to sweep across the country unhindered, stealing and destroying.

The situation grew more and more unbearable. One day a little Christian soldier - a Nazarene - disappeared from the ranks. We never saw him again, but we learned that his sister, a very young girl, had been forcibly taken by a Turkish officer of the Nazareth garrison. In Palestine, the dishonor of a girl can be redeemed by blood alone. The young soldier had hunted for his sister, found her in the barracks, and shot her; he then surrendered himself to the military authorities, who undoubtedly put him to death. He had not dared to kill the real criminal, - the officer, - for he knew that this would not only bring death to his family, but would call down terrible suffering on all the Christians of Nazareth.

When I learned of this tragedy, I determined to get out

of the army and return to my village at all costs. Nine Turkish officers out of ten can be bought, and I had reason to know that the officer in command at Saffêd was not that tenth man. Now, according to the law of the country, a man has the right to purchase exemption from military service for a sum equivalent to two hundred dollars. My case was different, for I was already enrolled; but everything is possible in Turkey. I set to work, and in less than two weeks I had bought half a dozen officers, ranging from corporal to captain, and had obtained consent of the higher authorities to my departure, provided I could get a physician's certificate declaring me unfit for service.

This was arranged in short order, although I am healthy-looking and the doctor found some difficulty in hitting on an appropriate ailment. Finally he decided that I had "too much blood" - whatever that might mean. With his certificate in hand, I paid the regular price of two hundred dollars from funds which had been sent me by my family, and walked out of the barracks a free man. My happiness was mingled with sadness at the thought of leaving the comrades with whom I had suffered and hoped. The four boys from my village were splendid. They felt that I was right in going home to do what I could for the people, but when they kissed me good-bye, in the Eastern fashion, the tears were running down their cheeks; and they were all strong, brave fellows.

On my way back to Zicron-Jacob, I passed through the town of Sheff'amr, where I got a foretaste of the conditions I was to find at home. A Turkish soldier, sauntering along the street, helped himself to fruit from the basket of an old vender, and went on without offering to pay a farthing. When the old man ventured to protest, the soldier turned like a flash and began beating him mercilessly, knocking him down and battering him until he was bruised, bleeding, and covered with the mud of the street. There was a hubbub; a crowd formed, through which a Turkish officer forced his way, demanding explanations. The soldier sketched the situation in a few words, whereupon the officer, turning to the old man, said impressively, - "If a soldier of the Sultan should choose to heap filth on your head, it is for you to kiss his hand in gratitude."

CHAPTER V

THE HIDDEN ARMS

When I finally reached Zicron-Jacob, I found rather a sad state of affairs. Military law had been declared. No one was supposed to be seen in the streets after sundown. The village was full of soldiers, and civilians had to put up with all kinds of ill-treatment. Moreover, our people were in a state of great excitement because an order had recently come from the Turkish authorities bidding them surrender whatever fire-arms or weapons they had in their possession. A sinister command, this: we knew that similar measures had been taken before the terrible Armenian massacres, and we felt that some such fate might be in preparation for our people. With the arms gone, the head men of the village knew that our last hold over the Arabs, our last chance for defense against sudden violence, would be gone, and they had refused to give them up. A house-to-house search had been made - fruitlessly, for our little arsenal was safely cached in a field, beneath growing grain.

It was a tense, unpleasant situation. At any time the Turks might decide to back up their demand by some of the violent methods of which they are past masters. A family council was held in my home, and it was decided to send my sister, a girl of twenty-three, to some friends at the American Syrian Protestant College at Beirut, so that we might be able to move freely without the responsibility of having a girl at home, in a country where, as a matter of course, the women-folk are seized and carried off before a massacre. At Beirut we knew that there was an American Consul-General, who kept in continual touch with the battleship anchored in the harbor for the protection of American interests.

My sister got away none too soon. One evening shortly after her departure, when I was standing in the doorway of our house watching the ever fresh miracle of the Eastern sunset, a Turkish officer came riding down the street with about thirty cavalrymen. He called me out and ordered me to follow him to the little village inn, where he dismounted and led me to one of the inner rooms, his spurs jingling loudly as we passed along the stone corridor.

I never knew whether I had been selected for this attention because of my prominence as a leader of the Jewish young men or simply because I had been standing conveniently in the doorway. The officer closed the door and came straight to the point by asking me where our store of arms was hidden. He was a big fellow, with the handsome, cruel features usual enough in his class. There was no open menace in his first question. When I refused to tell him, he began wheedling and offering all sorts of favors if I would betray my people. Then, all of a sudden, he whipped out a revolver and stuck the muzzle right in my face. I felt the blood leave my heart, but I was able to control myself and refuse his demand. The officer was not easily discouraged; the hours I passed in that little room, with its smoky kerosene lamp, were terrible ones. I realized, however, how tremendously important the question of the arms was, and strength was given me to hold out until the officer gave up in disgust and let me go home.

My father, an old man, knew nothing of what had happened, but the rest of my family were tremendously excited. I made light of the whole affair, but I felt sure that this was only the beginning. Sure enough, next morning - the Sabbath - the same officer returned and put three of the leading elders of the village, together with myself, under arrest. After another fruitless inquisition at the hotel, we were handcuffed and started on foot toward the prison, a day's journey away. As our little procession passed my home, my father, who was aged and feeble, came tottering forward to say good-bye to me. A soldier pushed him roughly back; he reeled, then fell full-length in the street before my eyes.

It was a dismal departure. We were driven through the streets shackled like criminals, and the women and children came out of the houses and watched us in silence - their heads bowed, tears running down their cheeks. They realized that for thirty-five years these old men, my comrades, had been struggling and suffering for their ideal - a regenerated Palestine; now, in the dusk of their life, it seemed as if all their hopes and dreams were coming to ruin. The oppressive tragedy of the situation settled down on me more and more heavily as the day wore on and heat and fatigue told on my companions. My feelings must have been written large on my face, for one of them, a fine-looking patriarch, tried to give me comfort by reminding me that we must not rely upon strength of arms, and that our spirit could never be broken, no

Alexander Aaronsohn

matter how defenseless we were. Thus he, an old man, was encouraging me instead of receiving help from my youth and enthusiasm.

At last we arrived at the prison and were locked into separate cells. That same night we were tortured with the *falagy*, or bastinado. The victim of this horrible punishment is trussed up, arms and legs, and thrown on his knees; then, on the bare soles of his feet a pliant green rod is brought down with all the force of a soldier's arm. The pain is exquisite; blood leaps out at the first cut, and strong men usually faint after thirty or forty strokes. Strange to say, the worst part of it is not the blow itself, but the whistling of the rod through the air as it rushes to its mark. The groans of my older comrades, whose gasps and prayers I could hear through the walls of the cell, helped me bear the agony until unconsciousness mercifully came to the rescue.

For several days more we were kept in the prison, sick and broken with suffering. The second night, as I lay sleepless and desperate on the strip of dirty matting that served as bed, I heard a scratch-scratching at the grated slit of a window, and presently a slender stick was inserted into the cell. I went over and shook it; some one at the other end was holding it firm. And then, a curious whispering sound began to come from the end of the stick. I put my ear down, and caught the voice of one of the men from our village. He had taken a long bamboo pole, pierced the joints, and crept up behind a broken old wall close beneath my window. By means of this primitive telephone we talked as long as we dared. I assured him that we were still enduring, and urged him on no account to give up the arms to the Turkish authorities - not even if we had to make the ultimate sacrifice.

Finally, when it was found that torture and imprisonment would not make us yield our secret, the Turks resorted to the final test - the ordeal which we could not withstand. They announced that on a certain date a number of our young girls would be carried off and handed over to the officers, to be kept until the arms were disclosed. We knew that they were capable of carrying out this threat; we knew exactly what it meant. There was no alternative. The people of our village had nothing to do but dig up the treasured arms and, with broken hearts, hand them over to the authorities.

And so the terrible news was brought to us one morning that we were free. Personally, I felt much happier on the day I was put in prison than when I was released. I had often wondered how our people had been able to bear the rack and thumbscrew of the Spanish Inquisition; but when my turn and my comrades' came for torture, I realized that the same spirit that helped our ancestors was working in us also.

Now I knew that our suffering had been useless. Whenever the Turkish authorities wished, the horrors of the Armenian massacres would live again in Zicron-Jacob, and we should be powerless to raise a hand to protect ourselves. As we came limping home through the streets of our village, I caught sight of my own Smith & Wesson revolver in the hands of a mere boy of fifteen - the son of a well-known Arab outlaw. I realized then that the Turks had not only taken our weapons, but had distributed them among the natives in order to complete our humiliation. The blood rushed to my face. I started forward to take the revolver away from the boy, but one of the old men caught hold of my sleeve and held me back.

CHAPTER VI

THE SUEZ CAMPAIGN

I have already spoken of the so-called "requisitioning" that took place among our people while I was working at Saffêd. This, of course, really amounted to whole-sale pillage. The hand of the Turkish looters had fallen particularly heavy on carts and draught animals. As the Arabs know little or nothing of carting, hauling, or the management of horses and mules, the Turks, simply enough, had "requisitioned" many of the owners - middle-aged or elderly men - and forced them to go south to help along with the tremendous preparations that were being made for the attack on Suez. Among these were a number of men from our village. In the course of time their families began to get the most harrowing messages from them. They were absolutely destitute, no wages being paid them by the Turks; their clothes were dropping off them in rags; many were sick. After much excited planning, it was decided to send another man and myself down south on a sort of relief expedition, with a substantial sum of money that had been raised with great difficulty by our people. Through the influence of my brother at the Agri-cultural Experiment Station, I got permission from the *mouchtar* to leave Zicron-Jacob, and about the middle of January, 1915, I set out for Jerusalem.

To Western minds, the idea of the Holy City serving as a base for modern military operations must be full of incongruities. And, as a matter of fact, it *was* an amazing sight to see the streets packed with khaki-clad soldiers and hear the brooding silence of ancient walls shattered by the crash of steel-shod army boots. Here, for the first time, I saw the German officers - quantities of them. Strangely out of place they looked, with their pink-and-whiteness that no amount of hot sunshine could quite burn off. They wore the regular German officer's uniform, except that the *Pickelhaube* was replaced by a khaki sun-helmet. I was struck by the youthfulness of them; many were nothing but boys, and there were weak, dissolute faces in plenty - a fact that was later explained when I heard that Palestine had been the dumping-ground for young men of high family whose parents were anxious to have them as far removed as possible from the danger zone. Fast's Hotel was the great meeting-place in Jerusalem for these young bloods. Every evening thirty or forty would foregather there to drink and talk women and strategy. I well remember the evening when one of them - a slender young Prussian with no back to his head, braceleted and monocled - rose and announced, in the decisive tones that go with a certain stage of intoxication: "What we ought to do is to hand over the organization of this campaign to Thomas Cook & Sons!"

However, the German officers were by no means all incompetents. They realized (I soon found out) that they had little hope of bringing a big army through the Egyptian desert and making a successful campaign there. Their object was to immobilize a great force of British troops around the Canal, to keep the Mohammedan population in Palestine impressed with

Turkish power, and to stir up religious unrest among the natives in Egypt. It must be admitted that in the first two of these purposes they have been successful.

The Turks were less far-sighted. They believed firmly that they were going to sweep the English off the face of the earth and enter Cairo in triumph, and preparations for the march on Suez went on with feverish enthusiasm. The ideas of the common soldiers on this subject were amusing. Some of them declared that the Canal was to be filled up by the sandbags which had been prepared in great quantities. Others held that thousands of camels would be kept without water for many days preceding the attack; then the thirsty animals, when released, would rush into the Canal in such numbers that the troops could march to victory over the packed masses of drowned bodies.

The army operating against Suez numbered about one hundred and fifty thousand men. Of these about twenty thousand were Anatolian Turks - trained soldiers, splendid fighting material, as was shown by their resistance at the Dardanelles. The rest were Palestinian Arabs, and very inferior troops they were. The Arab as a soldier is at once stupid and cunning: fierce when victory is on his side, but unreliable when things go against him. In command of the expedition was the famous Djemal Pasha, a Young Turk general of tremendous energy, but possessing small ability to see beyond details to the big, broad concepts of strategy. Although a great friend of Enver Pasha, he looked with disfavor on the German officers and, in particular, on Bach Pasha, the German Governor of Jerusalem, with whom he had serious disagreements. This dislike of the Germans was reflected among the lesser Turkish officers. Many of these, after long years of service, found themselves subordinated to young foreigners, who, in addition to arbitrary promotion, received much higher salaries than the Turks. What is more, they were paid in clinking gold, whereas the Turks, when paid at all, got paper currency.

Beersheba, a prosperous town of the ancient province of Idumea, was the southern base of operations for the advance on Suez. Some of our villagers had been sent to this district, and, in searching for them, I had the opportunity of seeing at least the taking-off place of the expedition. Beyond this point no Jew or Christian was allowed to pass, with the exception of the physicians, all of whom were non-Mohammedans who had been forced into the army.

Beersheba was swarming with troops. They filled the town and overflowed on to the sands outside, where a great tent-city grew up. And everywhere that the Turkish soldiers went, disorganization and inefficiency followed them. From all over the country the finest camels had been "requisitioned" and sent down to Beersheba until, at the time I was there, thousands and thousands of them were collected in the neighborhood. Through the laziness and stupidity of the Turkish commissariat officers, which no amount of German efficiency could counteract, no adequate provision was made for feeding them, and incredible numbers succumbed to starvation and neglect. Their great carcasses dotted the sand in all directions; it was only the wonderful antiseptic power of the Eastern sun that held pestilence in check.

The soldiers themselves suffered much hardship. The crowding in the tents was unspeakable; the water-supply was almost as inadequate as the medical service, which consisted chiefly of volunteer Red Crescent societies - among them a unit of twenty German nurses sent by the American College at Beirut. Medical supplies, such as they were, had been taken from the different mission hospitals and pharmacies of Palestine - these "requisitions" being made by officers who knew nothing of medical requirements and simply scooped together everything in sight. As a result, one of the army physicians told me that in Beersheba he had opened some medical chests consigned to him and found, to his horror, that they were full of microscopes and gynecological instruments - for the care of wounded soldiers in the desert!

Visits of British aeroplanes to Beersheba were common occurrences. Long before the machine itself could be seen, its whanging, resonant hum would come floating out of the blazing sky, seemingly from everywhere at once. Soldiers rushed from their tents, squinting up into the heavens until the speck was discovered, swimming slowly through the air; then followed wholesale firing at an impossible range until the officers forbade it. True to the policy of avoiding all unnecessary harm to the natives, these British aviators never dropped bombs on the town, but - what was more dangerous from the Turkish point of view - they would unload packages of pamphlets, printed in Arabic, informing the natives that they were being deceived; that the Allies were their only true friends; that the Germans were merely making use of them to further their own schemes, etc. These cleverly worded little tracts came showering down out of the sky, and at first they were eagerly picked up. The Turkish commanders, however, soon announced that any one found carrying them would pay the death penalty. After that, when the little bundles dropped near them, the natives would, run as if from high explosive bombs.

All things considered, it is wonderful that the Turkish demonstration against the Canal came as near to fulfillment as it did. Twenty thousand soldiers actually crossed the desert in six days on scant rations, and with them they took two big guns, which they dragged by hand when the mules dropped from thirst and exhaustion. They also carried pontoons to be used in crossing the Canal. Guns and pontoons are now at rest in the Museum at Cairo.

Just what took place in the attack is known to very few. The English have not seen fit to make public the details, and there was little to be got from the demoralized soldiers who returned to Beersheba. Piece by piece, however, I gathered that the attacking party had come up to the Canal at dawn. Finding everything quiet, they set about getting across, and had even launched a pontoon, when the British, who were lying in wait, opened a terrific fire from the farther bank, backed by armored locomotives and aeroplanes. "It was as if the gates of Jehannum were opened and its fires turned loose upon us," one soldier told me.

The Turks succeeded in getting their guns into action for a very short while. One of the men-of-war in the Canal was hit; several houses in Ismaïlia suffered damage; but the invaders were soon driven away in confusion, leaving perhaps two thousand prisoners in the hands of the English. If the latter had chosen to do so, they could have annihilated the Turkish forces then and there. The ticklish state of mind of the Mohammedan population in Egypt, however, has led them to adopt a policy of leniency and of keeping to the defensive, which subsequent developments have more than justified. It is characteristic of England's faculty for holding her colonies that batteries manned by Egyptians did the finest work in defense of the Canal.

The reaction in Palestine after the defeat at Suez was tremendous. Just before the attack, Djemal Pasha had sent out a telegram announcing the overwhelming defeat of the British vanguard, which had caused wild enthusiasm. Another later telegram proclaimed that the Canal had been reached, British men-of-war sunk, the Englishmen routed - with a loss to the Turks of five men and two camels, "which were afterwards recovered." "But," added the telegram, "a terrible sand-storm having arisen, the glorious army takes it as the wish of Allah not to continue the attack, and has therefore withdrawn in triumph."

These reports hoodwinked the ignorant natives for a little while, but when the stream of haggard soldiers, wounded and exhausted, began pouring back from the south, they guessed what had happened, and a fierce revulsion against the Germano-Turkish régime set in. A few weeks before the advance on Suez, I was in Jaffa, where the enthusiasm and excitement had been at fever-pitch. Parades and celebrations of all kinds in anticipation of the triumphal march into Egypt were taking place, and one day a camel, a dog, and a bull, decorated respectively with the flags of Russia, France, and England, were driven through the streets. The poor animals were horribly maltreated by the natives, who rained blows and flung filth upon them by way of giving concrete expression to their contempt for the Allies. Mr. Glazebrook, the American Consul at Jerusalem, happened to be with me in Jaffa that day; and never shall I forget the expression of pain and disgust on his face as he watched this melancholy little procession of scapegoats hurrying along the street.

Now, however, all was changed. The Arabs, who take defeat badly, turned against the authorities who had got them into such trouble. Rumors circulated that Djemal Pasha had been bought by the English and that the defeat at Suez had been planned by him, and persons keeping an ear close to the ground began to hear mutterings of a general massacre of Germans. In fact, things came within an ace of a bloody outbreak. I knew some Germans in Jaffa and Haifa who firmly believed that it was all over with them. In the defeated army itself the Turkish officers gave vent to their hatred of the Germans. Three German officers were shot by their Turkish comrades during the retreat, and a fourth committed suicide. However, Djemal Pasha succeeded in keeping order by means of stern repressive methods and by the fear roused by his large body-guard of faithful Anatolians.

We felt sure that the Turkish defeat would put a damper on the arrogance of the soldiery. But even the Mohammedan population were hoping that the Allies would push their victory and land troops in Syria and Palestine; for though they hated the infidel, they loved the Turk not at all, and the country was exhausted and the blockade of the Mediterranean by the Allies prevented the import and export of articles. The oranges were rotting on the trees because the annual Liverpool market was closed to Palestine, and other crops were in similar case. The country was short, too, of petroleum, sugar, rice, and other supplies, and even of matches. We had to go back to old customs and use flint and steel for fire, and we seldom used our lamps. Money was scarce, too, and, Turkey having declared a moratorium, cash was often unobtainable even by those who had money in the banks, and much distress ensued.

As the defeated army was pouring in from the south, I decided to leave Beersheba and go home. The roads and the fields were covered with dead camels and horses and mules. Hundreds of soldiers were straggling in disorder, many of them on leave but many deserting. Soon after the defeat at the Canal several thousand soldiers deserted, but an amnesty was declared and they returned to their regiments.

When I arrived at Jerusalem I found the city filled with soldiers. Djemal Pasha had just returned from the desert, and his quarters were guarded by a battery of two field guns. Nobody knew what to expect; some thought that the country would have a little more freedom now that the soldiery had lost its braggadocio, while others expected the lawlessness that attends disorganization. I went to see Consul Glazebrook. He is a true American, a Southerner, formerly a professor of theology at Princeton. He was most earnest and devoted in behalf of the American citizens that came under his care, rendering at Jerusalem the same sort of service that Ambassador Morgenthau has rendered at Constantinople. He was practically the only man who stood up for the poor, defenseless people of the city. He received me kindly, and I told him what I knew of conditions in the country, what I had heard among the Arabs, and of my own fears and apprehensions. He was visibly impressed and he advised me to see Captain Decker, of the U.S.S. Tennessee, who was then in Jaffa, promising to write himself to the captain of my proposed visit.

I went to Jaffa the same day and after two days' delay succeeded in seeing Captain Decker, with the further help of Mr. Glazebrook, who took me with him. The police interfered and tried to keep me from going aboard the ship, but after long discussions I was permitted to take my place in the launch that the captain had sent for the consul.

Captain Decker was interested in what I had to say, and at his request I dictated my story to his stenographer. What became of my report I do not know, - whether it was transmitted to the Department of State or whether Captain Decker communicated with Ambassador Morgenthau, - but at all events we soon began to see certain reforms inaugurated in parts of the country, and these reforms could have been effected only through pressure from Constantinople. The presence of the two American cruisers in the Mediterranean waters has without any doubt been instrumental in the saving of many lives.

CHAPTER VII

FIGHTING THE LOCUSTS

While I was traveling in the south, another menace to our people's welfare had appeared: the locusts. From the Soudan they came in tremendous hosts - black clouds of them that obscured the sun. It seemed as if Nature had joined in the conspiracy against us. These locusts were of the species known as the pilgrim, or wandering, locust; for forty years they had not come to Palestine, but now their visitation was like that of which the prophet Joel speaks in the Old Testament. They came full-grown, ripe for breeding; the ground was covered with the females digging in the soil and depositing their egg-packets, and we knew that when they hatched we should be overwhelmed, for there was not a foot of ground in which these eggs were not to be found.

The menace was so great that even the military authorities were obliged to take notice of it. They realized that if it were allowed to fulfill itself, there would be famine in the land, and the army would suffer with the rest. Djemal Pasha summoned my brother (the President of the Agricultural Experiment Station at Athlit) and intrusted him with the organization of a campaign against the insects. It was a hard enough task. The Arabs are lazy, and fatalistic besides; they cannot understand why men should attempt to fight the *Djesh Allah* ("God's Army"), as they call the locusts. In addition, my brother was seriously handicapped by lack of petroleum, galvanized iron, and other articles which could not be obtained because of the Allies' blockade.

In spite of these drawbacks, however, he attempted to work up a scientific campaign. Djemal Pasha put some thousands of Arab soldiers at his disposition, and these were set to work digging trenches into which the hatching locusts were driven and destroyed. This is the only means of coping with the situation: once the locusts get their wings, nothing can be done with them. It was a hopeless fight. Nothing short of the coöperation of every farmer in the country could have won the day; and while the people of the progressive Jewish villages struggled on to the end, - men, women, and children working in the fields until they were exhausted, - the Arab farmers sat by with folded hands. The threats of the military authorities only stirred them to half-hearted efforts. Finally, after two months of toil, the campaign was given up and the locusts broke in waves over the countryside, destroying everything. As the prophet Joel said, "The field is wasted, the land mourneth; for the corn is wasted: the new wine is dried up, the oil languisheth.... The land is as the garden of Eden before them, and behind them a desolate wilderness."

Not only was every green leaf devoured, but the very bark was peeled from the trees, which stood out white and lifeless, like skeletons. The fields were stripped to the ground, and the old men of our villages, who had given their lives to cultivating these gardens and vineyards, came out of the synagogues where they had

Alexander Aaronsohn

been praying and wailing, and looked on the ruin with dimmed eyes. Nothing was spared. The insects, in their fierce hunger, tried to engulf everything in their way. I have seen Arab babies, left by their mothers in the shade of some tree, whose faces had been devoured by the oncoming swarms of locusts before their screams had been heard. I have seen the carcasses of animals hidden from sight by the undulating, rustling blanket of insects. And in the face of such a menace the Arabs remained inert. With their customary fatalism they accepted the locust plague as a necessary evil. They could not understand why we were so frantic to fight it. And as a matter of fact, they really got a good deal out of the locusts, for they loved to feast upon the female insects. They gathered piles of them and threw them upon burning charcoal, then, squatting around the fire, devoured the roasted insects with great gusto. I saw a fourteen-year-old boy eat as many as a hundred at a sitting.

CHAPTER VIII

THE LEBANON

During the locust invasion my brother sent me on an inspection tour to investigate the ravages of the insect in Syria. With an official *boyouroulton* (passport) in my pocket, I was able to travel all over the country without being interfered with by the military authorities. I had an excellent opportunity to see what was going on everywhere. The locusts had destroyed everything from as far south as the Egyptian desert to the Lebanon Mountains on the north; but the locust was not the only, nor the worst, plague that the people had to complain of. The plundering under the name of "military requisitions," the despotic rule of the army officers, and the general insecurity were even more desolating.

As I proceeded on my journey northward, I hoped to find consolation and brighter prospects in the independent province of the Lebanon. Few Americans know just what the Lebanon is. From the repeated allusions in the Bible most people imagine it to be nothing but a mountain. The truth is that a beautiful province of about four thousand square miles bears that name. The population of the Lebanon consists of a Christian sect called Maronites and the Druses, the latter a people with a secret religion the esoteric teachings of which are known only to the initiated, and never divulged to outsiders. Both these peoples are sturdy, handsome folk. Through the machinations of the Turks, whose policy is always to "divide and rule," the Maronites were continually fighting against the Druses. In 1860 Turkish troops joined with the Druses and fell upon the Maronites with wholesale massacres that spread as far south as Damascus, where ten thousand Christians were killed in two days.

The European powers were moved at last. Fifty warships were sent to Beirut, and ten thousand French troops were landed in the Lebanon, to create order. Under the pressure of the European powers the Sublime Porte was forced to grant an autonomy for the province of the Lebanon. The French, English, German, Russian, Austrian, and, a year later, the Italian, Governments were signing the guaranty of this autonomy.

Since then the Lebanon has had peace. The Governor of the province must always be a Christian, but the General Council of the Lebanon includes representatives of all the different races and religions of the population. A wonderful development began with the liberation from Turkish oppression. Macadamized roads were built all over the province, agriculture was improved, and there was complete safety for life and property. There is a proverb now in Palestine and Syria which says, "In the Lebanon a virgin may travel alone at midnight and be safe, and a purse of gold dropped in the road at midday will never be stolen." And the proverb told the literal truth.

When one crossed the boundary from Turkish Palestine into the Lebanon province, what a change met his eyes! - peaceful and prosperous villages, schools filled with children, immense plantations of mulberry trees and olives, the slopes of the mountains terraced with beautiful vineyards, a handsome and sturdy population, police on every road to help the stranger, and young girls and women with happy laugh and chatter working in the fields. With a population of about six hundred thousand this province exported annually two million dollars' worth of raw silk, silkworm-raising being a specialty of the Lebanon.

When autonomy was granted the Lebanon, French influence became predominant among the Maronites and other Christians of the province. French is spoken by almost all of them, and love for France is a deep-rooted sentiment of the people. On the other hand, the Druses feel the English influence. For the last sixty years England has been the friend of the Druses, and they have not forgotten it.

It may be worth while to tell in a few words the story of one man who accomplished wonders in spreading the influence of his country. Sir Richard Wood was born in London, a son of Catholic parents. From his early boyhood he aspired to enter the diplomatic service. The East attracted him strongly, and in order to learn Arabic he went with another young English-man to live in the Lebanon. In Beirut they sought the hospitality of the Maronite patriarch. For a few days they were treated with lavish hospitality, and then the patriarch summoned them before him and told them that they must leave the city within twenty-four hours. The reason for their disgrace they discovered later. Not suspecting that they were being put to the test, they had eaten meat on a Friday, and this made the patriarch think that they were not true Catholics, but were there as spies.

Leaving Beirut in haste, Wood and his friend sought shelter with the Druses, who received them with open arms. For two years Wood lived among the Druses, in the village of Obey. There he learned Arabic and became thoroughly acquainted with the country and with the ways of the Druses, and there he conceived the idea of winning the Druses for England to counteract the influence of the French Maronites. He went back to London, where he succeeded in impressing his views upon the Foreign Office, and he returned to Syria charged with a secret mission. Before long he persuaded the Druse chieftains to address a petition to England asking for British protection.

British protection was granted, and for over thirty years Richard Wood, virtually single-handed, shaped the destiny of Syria. It was he who broke the power of Ibrahim Pasha, the son of Mehemet Ali; it was he who guided Admiral Stopford in the bombardment of Beirut; it was he, again, who brought about the landing of English troops in Syria in 1841; we find him afterwards in Damascus as British Consul, and wherever he went he was always busy spreading English power and prestige. He understood the East thoroughly and felt that England must be strong in Syria if she wished to retain her imperial power. It is very unfortunate that the policy of Sir Richard Wood was not carried out by his nation.

It was with high hopes and expectations that I approached the Lebanon. I was looking forward to the moment when I should find myself among people who were free from the Turkish yoke, in a country where I should be able to breathe freely for a few hours.

But how great was my consternation, when, on entering the Lebanon, I found on all the roads Turkish soldiers who stopped me every minute to ask for my papers! Even then I could not realize that the worst had happened. Of course, rumors of the Turkish occupation of the Lebanon had reached us a few weeks before, but we had not believed it, as we knew that Germany and Austria were among those who guaranteed the autonomy of the Lebanon. It was true, however; the scrap of paper that guaranteed the freedom of the Lebanon had proved of no more value to the Lebanese than had that other scrap of paper to Belgium. As I entered the beautiful village of Ed-Damur, one of the most prosperous and enchanting places on earth, I saw entire regiments of Turkish troops encamped in and about the village.

While I was watering my horse, I tried to ask questions from a few inhabitants. My fair hair and complexion and my khaki costume made them take me for a German, and they barely answered me, but when I addressed them in French their faces lit up. For the Lebanon, for all it is thousands of miles away from France, is nevertheless like a French province. For fifty years the French language and French culture have taken hold of the Lebanon. No Frenchman has more love for and faith in France than lie in the hearts of the Lebanese Christians. They have never forgotten that when massacres were threatening to wipe out all the Christians of the Lebanon, ten thousand French soldiers swept over the mountains to spread peace, life, and French gayety.

And when the poor people heard the language they loved, and when they found out that I too was the son of an oppressed and ruined community, all the sadness and bitterness of their hearts was told me, - how the Turkish soldiers had spread over the beloved mountains of Lebanon; how the strong, stalwart young Lebanese had been taken away from the mountains and forced into the Turkish army; how the girls and women were hiding in their homes, afraid to be seen by the soldiers and their officers; how the chieftains were imprisoned and even hanged; and how violence and pillage had spread over the peaceful country.[Footnote: Since the above was written the American press has chronicled many atrocities committed in the Lebanon. The execution of leaders and the complete blockade of the mountains by the Turkish authorities resulted in the starving of eighty thousand Lebanese. The French Government has warned Turkey through the American Ambassador that the Turks will be held accountable for their deeds.]

I could not help wondering at the mistakes of the Allies. If they had understood the situation in Palestine and Syria, how differently this war might have eventuated! The Lebanon and Syria would have raised a hundred thousand picked men, if the Allies had landed in Palestine. The Lebanon would have fought for its independence as heroically as did the Belgians. Even the Arab population would have welcomed the Allies as liberators. But alas!

With a saddened heart I pursued my journey into Beirut. My coming was a joyful surprise to my sister. Many sad things had happened since she had last seen me. During my imprisonment she had suffered tortures, not knowing what would happen to me, and now that she saw me alive she cried from happiness. She told me how kindly she had been treated by President Bliss, of the Syrian Protestant College, and of all the good things the college had done.

What a blessing the college was for the people of Beirut! Many unfortunate people were saved from prison and hardships through the intervention of President Bliss. He never tired of rendering service, wonderful personal service. But alas, even his influence and power began to wane. The American prestige in the country was broken, and the Turkish Government no longer respected the American flag. An order issued from Constantinople demanded that the official language of the college be Turkish instead of English, and Turkish officers even dared to enter the college premises to search for citizens belonging to the belligerent nations, without troubling to ask permission from the American Consul.

CHAPTER IX

A ROBBER BARON OF PALESTINE

Beirut is a city of about two hundred thousand inhabitants, half of whom are Christians and the rest Mohammedans and Jews. The pinch of hunger was already felt there. Bread was to be had only on tickets issued by the Government, and prices in general were extremely high. The population were discontented and turbulent, and every day thousands of women came before the governor's residence to cry and protest against the scarcity of bread.

The Allies' warships often passed near the town, but the people were not afraid of them, for it was known that the Allies had no intention of bombarding the cities. Only once had a bombardment taken place. Toward the end of March, 1915, a French warship approached the bay of Haifa and landed an officer with a letter to the commandant of that town giving notice of his intention to bombard the German Consulate at 3 P.M. sharp. This was in retaliation for the propaganda carried on by the consul, Leutweld von Hardegg, and chiefly because of his desecration of the grave of Bonaparte's soldiers. The consul had time to pack up his archives and valuables, and he left his house before three. The bombardment began exactly at three. Fifteen shells were fired with a wonderful precision. Not one house in the neighborhood of the consulate was touched, but the consulate itself was a heap of ruins after a few shells had struck it. The population was exceedingly calm. Only the German colony was panic-stricken, and on every German house an American flag was raised. It was rather humorous to see all the Germans who were active in the Turkish army in one capacity or another seek safety by means of this trick.

This bombardment had a sobering effect upon the Mohammedan population. They saw that the Allies were not wholly ignorant of what was going on in the country and that they could retaliate, and safety for the non-Mohammedans increased accordingly.

In general Beirut was a rather quiet and safe place. The presence of an American cruiser in the port had much to do with that. The American sailors were allowed to come ashore three times a week, and they spent their money lavishly. It was estimated that Beirut was getting more than five thousand dollars a week out of them. But the natives were especially impressed by the manliness and quick action of the American boys. Frequently a few sailors were involved in a street fight with scores of Arabs, and they always held their own. In a short time the Americans became feared, which in the Orient is equivalent to saying they were respected. The Beirut people are famous for their fighting spirit, but this spirit was not manifested after a few weeks of intimate acquaintance with the American blue-jackets.

My inspection of the devastation caused by the locusts completed, I returned home. The news that greeted me there was alarming. I must narrate with some detail the events which finally decided me to leave the country. About one hour's ride on horseback from our village lives a family of Turkish nobles, the head of which was Sadik Pasha, brother of the famous Kiamil Pasha, several times Grand Vizier of the Empire. Sadik, who had been exiled from Constantinople, came to Palestine and bought great tracts of land near my people. After his death his sons - good-for-nothing, wild fellows - were forced to sell most of the estate - all except one Fewzi Bey, who retained his part of the land and lived on it. Here he collected a band of friends as worthless as himself and gradually commenced a career of plundering and "frightfulness" much like that of the robber barons of mediaeval Germany. Before the outbreak of the war he confined his attentions chiefly to the Arabs, whom he treated shamefully. He raided cattle and crops and carried off girls and women in broad daylight. On one occasion he stopped a wedding procession and carried off the young bride. Then he seized the bridegroom, against whom he bore a grudge, and subjected the poor Bedouin to the bastinado until he consented to divorce his wife by pronouncing the words, "I divorce thee," three times in the presence of witnesses, according to Mohammedan custom. This Bedouin was the grandson of the Sheikh Hilou, a holy man of the region upon whose grave the Arabs are accustomed to make their prayers. But we villagers of Zicron-Jacob had never submitted to Fewzi Bey in any way; our young men were organized and armed, and after a few encounters he let us alone.

After the mobilization, however, and the taking away of our arms, this outlaw saw that his chance had come. He began to send his men and his camels into our fields to harvest our crops and carry them off. This pillage continued until the locusts came - Fewzi, in the mean while, becoming so bold that he would gallop through the streets of our village with his horsemen, shooting right and left into the air and insulting old men and women. He boasted - apparently with reason - that the authorities at Haifa were powerless to touch him.

There was one hope left. Djemal Pasha had boasted that he had introduced law and order; the country was under military rule; it remained to see what he would say and do when the crimes of Fewzi Bey were brought to his notice. Accordingly, armed with my *boyouroulton*, or passport, of a locust-inspector, I rode to Jerusalem, where I procured, through my brother, who was then in favor, an interview with Djemal Pasha. He received me on the very day of my arrival, and listened attentively while for a whole hour I poured out the story of Fewzi Bey's outrages. I put my whole heart into the plea and wound up by asking if it was to the credit of the progressive Young Turks to shelter feudal abuses of a bygone age. Djemal seemed to be impressed. He sprang from his chair, began walking up and down the room; then with a great dramatic gesture he exclaimed, "Justice shall be rendered!" and assured me that a commission of army officers would be sent at once to start an investigation. I returned to Zicron-Jacob with high hopes.

Sure enough, a few days later Fewzi Bey was summoned to Jerusalem; at the same time the "commission," which had dwindled to one single officer on secret mission, put in an appearance and began to make inquiries among the natives. He got little satisfaction at first, for they lived in mortal terror of the outlaw; they grew bolder, however, when they learned his purpose. Complaints and testimonies came pouring in, and in four days the officer had the names of hundreds of witnesses, establishing no less than fifty-two crimes of the most serious nature. Fewzi's friends and relatives, in the mean while, were doing their utmost to stem the tide of accusations. The Kaimakam (lieutenant-governor) of Haifa came in person to our village and threatened the elders with all sorts of severities if they did not retract the charges they had made. But they stood firm. Had not Djemal Pasha, commander-in-chief of the armies in Palestine, given his word of honor that we should have redress?

We were soon shown the depth of our naïveté in fancying that justice could be done in Turkey by a Turk. Fewzi Bey came back from Jerusalem, not in convict's clothes, but in the uniform of a Turkish officer! Djemal Pasha had commissioned him commandant of the Moujahaddeen (religious militia) of the entire region! It was bad enough to stand him as an outlaw; now we had to submit to him as an officer. He came riding into our village daily, ordering everybody about and picking me out for distinguished spitefulness.

My position soon became unbearable. I was, of course, known as the organizer of the young men's union which for so long had put up a spirited resistance to Fewzi; I was still looked upon as a leader of the younger spirits, and I knew that sooner or later Fewzi would try to make good his threat, often repeated, that he would "shoot me like a dog." It was hardly likely that an open attempt on my life would be made. When Ambassador Morgenthau visited Palestine, he had stayed in our village and given my family the evidence of his sincere friendship. These things count in the East, and I soon got the reputation of having influential friends. However, there were other ways of disposing of me. One evening, about sunset, while I was riding through a valley near our village, my horse shied violently in passing a clump of bushes. I gave him the spur and turned and rode toward the bushes just in time to see a horseman dash out wildly with a rifle across his saddle. I kept the incident to myself, but I was more cautious and kept my eyes open wherever I went. One afternoon, a fortnight later, as I was riding to Hedera, another Jewish village, two hours' ride away, a shot was fired from behind a sand-dune. The bullet burned a hole in the lapel of my coat.

That night I had a long talk with my brother. There was no doubt whatever in his mind that I should try to leave the country, while I, on the contrary, could not bear to think of deserting my people at the crisis of their fortunes. It was a beautiful night, such a night, I think, as only Palestine can show, a white, serene, moon-bathed night. The roar of the Mediterranean came out of the stillness as if to remind us that help and salvation could come only from the sea, the sea upon which scores of the warships of the Allies were sailing back and forth. We had argued into the small hours before I yielded to his persuasion.

CHAPTER X

A RASH ADVENTURE

It was all very well to decide to leave the country; to get safely away was a different matter. There were two ways out. One of these - the land route by Constantinople - could not be considered. The other way was to board one of the American cruisers which, by order of Ambassador Morgenthau, were empowered to assist citizens of neutral countries to leave the Ottoman Empire. These cruisers had already done wonderful rescue work for the Russian Jews in Palestine, who, when war was declared, were to have been sent to the Mesopotamian town of Urfa - there to suffer massacre and outrage like the Armenians. This was prevented by Mr. Morgenthau's strenuous representations, with the result that these Russian Jews were gathered together as in a great drag-net and herded to Jaffa, amidst suffering unspeakable. There they were met by the American cruisers which were to transport them to Egypt. Up to the very moment when they set foot on the friendly warships they were robbed and horribly abused by the Jaffa boatmen. The eternal curse of the Wandering Jew! Driven from Russia, they come to seek shelter in Turkey; Turkey then casts them from her under pretext that they are loyal to Russia. Truly, the Jew lifts his eyes to the mountains, asking the ancient and still unanswered question, "Whence shall come my help?"

The Turkish Government later repented of its leniency in allowing these Russian Jews to escape, and gave orders that only neutrals should leave the country - and then only under certain conditions. I was not a neutral; my first papers of American citizenship were valueless to further my escape. I had heard, however, that the United States cruiser Tennessee was to call at Jaffa, and I determined to get aboard her by hook or by crook. One evening, as soon as darkness had fallen, I bade a sorrowful farewell to my people, and set off for Jaffa, traveling only by night and taking out-of-the-way paths to avoid the pickets, for now that the locust campaign was over, my *boyouroulton* was useless. At dawn, two days later, I slipped into Jaffa by way of the sand-dunes and went to the house of a friend whom I could trust to help me in every possible way, and begged him to find me a passport for a neutral. He set off in search and I waited all day at his house, consumed with impatience and anxiety. At last, toward evening, my friend returned, but the news he brought was not cheering. He had found a passport, indeed, but his report of the rigors of the inspection at the wharf was such as to make it clear that the chances of my getting through on a false passport were exceedingly slim, since I was well known in Jaffa. If I were caught in such an undertaking, it might mean death for me and punishment for the friends who had helped me.

Evidently this plan was not feasible. All that night I racked my brain for a solution. Finally I decided to stake everything on what appeared to be my only chance. The Tennessee was due on the next day but one, early in the morning. I gave my friend the name of a boatman who was under obligations to me and had sworn to be my friend for life or death. Even under the circumstances I hesitated to trust a Mohammedan, but it seemed the only thing to do; I had no choice left. My friend brought the boatman, and I put my plan before him, appealing to his daring and his sense of honor. I wanted him to take me at midnight in his fishing-boat from an isolated part of the coast and wait for the appearance of the Tennessee; then, on her arrival, amid the scramble of boats full of refugees, I was to jump aboard, while he would return with the other boats. The poor fellow tried to remonstrate, pointing out the dangers and what he called - rightly enough, doubtless - the folly of the plan. I stuck to it, however, making it clear that his part would be well paid for, and at last he consented and we arranged a meeting-place behind the sand-dunes by the shore.

I put a few personal belongings into a little suit-case and had my friend give it to one of the refugees who was to sail on the Tennessee. If I succeeded, I was to recover it when we reached Egypt. The only thing I took with me was the paper which declared my "intention of becoming an American citizen," the "first paper." From this document I was determined not to part. I shall not tell how I kept it on me, as the means I used may still be used by others in concealing such papers and a disclosure of the secret might bring disaster to them. Suffice it to say that I had the paper with me and that no search would have brought it to light.

Arrived next morning at the appointed place, I gave the signal agreed upon, the whine of a jackal, and, after repeating it again and again, I heard a very low and muffled answer. My boatman was there! I had some fear that he might have betrayed me and that I should presently see a soldier or policeman leap out of the little boat, but my fears proved groundless, the man was faithful.

We rowed out quietly, our boat a little nutshell on the tossing waves. But I was relieved; the elements did not frighten me; on the contrary, I felt secure and refreshed in the midst of the sea. When morning began to dawn, scores of little boats came out of the harbor and circled about waiting for the cruiser. This was our chance. I crouched in the bottom of our boat and to all appearances my boatman was engaged merely in fishing. After I had lain there over an hour with my heart beating like a drum and with small hopes for the success of my undertaking, I heard at last the whistle of the approaching cruiser followed by a Babel of mad shouting and cursing among the boatmen. In the confusion I felt it safe to sit up. No one paid the slightest attention to me. All were engaged in a wild race to reach and mount the Tennessee's ladder. I scrambled up with the rest, and when, on the deck, an officer demanded my passport, I put on a bold front and asked him to tell Captain Decker that Mr. Aaronsohn wished to see him.

Ten minutes later I stood in the captain's cabin. There I unfolded my story, and wound up by asking him if, under the circumstances, my "first papers" might not entitle me to protection. As I spoke I could see the struggle that was going on within him. When he answered it was to explain, with the utmost kindness, that if he took me aboard his ship it would be to forfeit his word of honor to the Turkish Government, his pledge to take only citizens of neutral countries; that he could not consider me an American on the strength of my first papers; and that any such evasion might lead to serious complications for him and for his Government. Well, there was nothing for me to do but to withdraw and go back to Jaffa to face trial for an attempt to escape.

When I reached the deck again I found it swarming with refugees, many of whom knew me and came up to congratulate me on getting away. I could only shake my head and with death in my heart descend the Tennessee's ladder. It did not matter now what boat I took. Any boatman was eager enough to take me for a few cents. As I sat in the boat, every stroke of the oars bringing me nearer to the shore and to what I felt was inevitable captivity, a great bitterness swelled my heart. I was tired, utterly tired of all the dangers and trials I had been going through for the last months. From depression I sank into despair and out of despair came, strange to say, a great serenity, the serenity of despair.

On the quay I ran into Hassan Bey, commandant of the police, who was superintending the embarkation of refugees. I knew him and he knew me. Half an hour later I was in police headquarters under examination by Hassan Bey. I was desperate, and answered him recklessly. A seasick man is indifferent to shipwreck. This was the substance of our conversation: -

"How did you get aboard the ship?"

"In a boat with some refugees. A woman hid me with her skirts."

"So you were trying to escape, were you?"

"If I had been, I shouldn't have come back."

"Then what did you do on the cruiser?"

"I went to talk to the captain, who is a friend of mine. My life is in danger. Fewzi Bey is after me, and I wanted *my friends in America* to know how justice is done in Palestine."

"Who are your friends in America?"

"Men who could break you in a minute."

"Do you know to whom you are speaking?"

"Yes, Hassan Bey. I am sick of persecution. I wish you would hang me with your own hands as you hanged the young Christian; my friends would have your life for mine."

I wonder now how I dared to speak to him in this manner. But the bluff carried. Hassan Bey looked at me curiously for a moment - then smiled and offered me a cigarette, assuring me that he believed me a loyal citizen, and declaring he felt deeply hurt that I had not come to him for permission to visit the cruiser. We parted with a profusion of Eastern compliments, and that evening I started back to Zicron-Jacob.

CHAPTER XI

ESCAPE

The failure of my attempt to leave the country only sharpened my desire to make another trial. The danger of the enterprise tended to reconcile me to deserting my family and comrades and seeking safety for myself. As I racked my brain for a promising plan, a letter came from my sister in Beirut with two pieces of news which were responsible for my final escape. The American College was shortly to close for the summer, and the U.S.S. Chester was to sail for Alexandria with refugees aboard. Beirut is a four days' trip from our village, and roads are unsafe. It was out of the question to permit my sister to come home alone, and it was impossible for any of us to get leave to go after her; nor did we want to have her at home in the unsettled condition of the country. I began wondering if I could not possibly get to Beirut and get my sister aboard the Chester, which offered, perhaps, the last opportunity to go out with the refugees. It would be a difficult undertaking but it might be our only chance and I quickly made up my mind to carry it out if it were a possible thing. I had to act immediately; no time was to be lost, for no one could tell how soon the Chester might sail.

My last adventure had been entered upon with forebodings, but now I felt that I should succeed. To us

Orientals intuition speaks in very audible tones and we are trained from childhood to listen to its voice. It was with a feeling of confidence in the outcome, therefore, that I bade this second good-bye to my family and dearest friends. Solemn hours they were, these hours of farewell, hours that needed few words. Then once more I slipped out into the night to make my secret way to Beirut.

It was about midnight when I left home, dressed in a soldier's uniform and driving a donkey before me. I traveled only by night and spent each day in hiding in some cave or narrow valley where I could sleep with some measure of security. For food I had brought bread, dried figs, and chocolate, and water was always to be found in little springs and pools. In these clear, warm nights I used to think of David, a fugitive and pursued by his enemies. How well I could now understand his despairing cry: "How long wilt thou forget me, O Lord? for ever?... How long shall mine enemy be exalted over me?"

Five nights I journeyed, and at last one morning beautiful Beirut appeared in the distance and I found myself in the forest of pines that leads into the city. The fresh dawn was filled with the balmy breath of the pines and all the odors of the Lebanon. Driving my donkey before me, I boldly approached the first picket-house and saluted the non-commissioned officer in military fashion. He stopped me and asked whence I came and where I was going. I smiled sweetly and replied that I was the orderly of a German officer who was surveying the country a few hours to the south and that I was going to Beirut for provisions. Then I lighted a cigarette and sat down for a chat. After discussing politics and the war for a few minutes, I jumped up, exclaiming that if I didn't hurry I should be late, and so took my departure. It was all so simple, and it brought me safely to Beirut. My donkey, having served the purpose for which I had brought him, was speedily abandoned, and I hurried to a friend's house, where I exchanged my uniform for the garb of a civilian.

My sister was the most surprised person on earth when she saw me walking into her room, and, when I told her that I wanted her to go with me on the Chester, she thought me crazy, for she knew that hundreds of persons were trying in vain to find means of leaving the country and it seemed to her impossible that we, who were Turkish subjects, could succeed in outwitting the authorities. Even when I had explained my plans and she was willing to admit the possibility of success, she still felt doubts as to whether it would be right for her to leave the country while her friends were left behind in danger. I assured her, however, that our family would feel relieved to know that we were in safety and could come back fresh and strong after the war to help in rebuilding the country.

Having gained her consent, I still had the difficult problem of ways and means before me. The Chester had orders to take citizens of neutral countries only. Passports had to be examined by the Turkish authorities and by the American Consul-General, who gave the final permission to board the cruiser. How was I to pass this double scrutiny? After long and arduous search, with the assistance of several good friends, I at last discovered a man who was willing to sell me the passports of a young couple belonging to a neutral nation. I cannot go into particulars about this arrangement, of course. Suffice it to say that my sister was to travel as my wife and that we both had to disguise ourselves so as to answer the descriptions on the passports. When I went to the American Consulate-General to get the permit, I found the building crowded with people of all nations, - Spanish and Greek and Dutch and Swiss, - all waiting for the precious little papers that should take them aboard the American cruiser, that haven of liberty and safety. The Chester was to take all these people to Alexandria, and those who had the means were to be charged fifty cents a day for their food. From behind my dark goggles I recognized many a person in disguise like myself and seeking escape. We never betrayed recognition for fear of the spies who infested the place.

After securing my permit, I ran downstairs and straight to "my" consul, whose dragoman I took along with me to the *seraya*, or government building. Of course, the dragoman was well tipped and he helped me considerably in hastening the examination I had to undergo at the hands of the Turkish officials. All went well, and I hurried back to my sister triumphant.

The Chester was to sail in two days, but while we were waiting, the alarming news came that the American Consul had been advised that the British Government refused to permit the landing of the refugees in Egypt and that the departure of the Chester was indefinitely postponed. With a sinking at my heart I rushed up to the American Consulate for details and there learned that the U.S.S. Des Moines was to sail in a few hours for Rhodes with Italian and Greek refugees and that I could go on her if I wished. In a few minutes I had my permit changed for the trip on the Des Moines and I hurried home to my sister. We hastily got together the few belongings we were to take with us, jumped into a carriage, and drove to the harbor.

We had still another ordeal to go through. My sister was taken into a private room and thoroughly searched; so was I. Nobody could leave the country with more than twenty-five dollars in cash on his person. Our baggage was carefully overhauled. No papers or books could be taken. My sister's Bible was looked upon with much suspicion since it contained a map of ancient Canaan. I explained that this was necessary for the orientation of our prayers and that without it we could not tell in which direction to turn our faces when praying! This seemed plausible to the Moslem examiners and saved the Bible, the only book we now possess as a souvenir from home. Now our passports were examined again and several questions were asked. My sister was brave and self-possessed, cool and unconcerned in manner, and at last the final signature was affixed and we jumped into the little boat that was to take us out to the ship.

At this moment a man approached, a dry-goods dealer of whom my sister had made some purchases a few months before. He seemed to recognize her and he asked her in German if she were not Miss Aaronsohn. I felt my blood leave my face, and, looking him straight in the eye, I whispered, "If you say one word more, you will be a dead man; so help me God!" He must have felt that I meant exactly what I said, for he walked off mumbling unintelligibly.

At last the boat got away, and five minutes later we were mounting the side of the Des Moines. Throngs of refugees covered the decks of the cruiser. Their faces showed tension and anxiety. Their presence there seemed too good to be true, and all awaited the moment when the ship should heave anchor. A Filipino sailor showed us about, and as he spoke Italian, I told him I wanted to be hidden somewhere till the ship got under way. I felt that even yet we were not entirely safe. That my fears were justified I discovered shortly, when from our hiding-place I saw the shopkeeper approaching in a small boat with a Turkish officer. They looked over all the refugees on the deck, but searched for us in vain. After a half-hour more of uncomfortable tension the engines began to sputter, the propellers revolved, and - we were safe!

The day was dying and a beautiful twilight softened the outlines of the Lebanon and the houses of Beirut. The Mediterranean lay quiet and peaceful around us, and the healthy, sturdy American sailors gave a feeling of confidence. As the cruiser drew out of the harbor, a great cry of farewell arose from the refugees on board, a cry in which was mingled the relief of being free, anguish at leaving behind parents and friends, fear and hope for the future. A little later the sailors were lined up in arms to salute the American flag when it was lowered for the night. Moved by a powerful instinct of love and respect, all the refugees jumped to their feet, the men bareheaded and the women with folded hands, and in that moment I understood as I had never understood before the real sacred meaning of a flag. To all those people standing in awe about that piece of cloth bearing the stars and stripes America was an incarnation of love universal, of freedom and salvation.

The cool Syrian night, our first night on the cruiser, was spent in songs, hymns, and conversation. We were all too excited to sleep. Friends discovered friends and tales of woe were exchanged, stories of hardship, injustice, oppression, all of which ended with mutual congratulations on escaping from the clutches of the Turks.

Alexander Aaronsohn

www.ingramcontent.com/pod-product-compliance
Lightning Source LLC
Chambersburg PA
CBHW030112070426
42448CB00036B/750